T0194848

THOUGHTS FOR YOUR DAY

MEDITATIONS FOOD FOR CONTEMPLATION

Marcus A. Roberts

authorHOUSE®

AuthorHouse™
1663 Liberty Drive
Bloomington, IN 47403
www.authorhouse.com
Phone: 1 (800) 839-8640

Published by AuthorHouse 10/22/2019

ISBN: 978-1-7283-3254-3 (sc)
ISBN: 978-1-7283-3255-0 (hc)
ISBN: 978-1-7283-3253-6 (e)

Print information available on the last page.

Marcus Aurelius made a profound statement when he said, "A man's life is what his thoughts make of it." We know that this timeless wisdom applies to the human race the world over. With that statement in mind, I dedicate this book to people who seek to matriculate through the Thought Knowledge College to improve the quality of their lives through the conscious endeavor of possibility thinking.

Contents

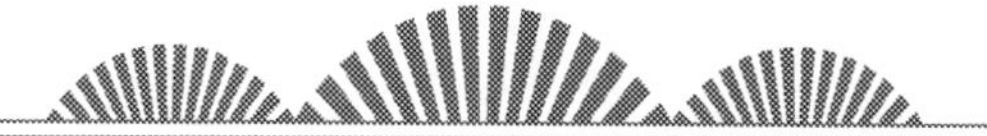

ACKNOWLEDGMENTS

To all those that encouraged me along the way to dream big and live deeply! To my best friend and college football teammate and roommate Christopher Houston, keep building bridges and empowering future generations!

INTRODUCTION

It is my personal belief that there is a segment of the population that subscribes to the inerrant and infallible word of God contained in the timeless wisdom endemic in the biblical scriptures, while embracing the humanistic wisdom of movers in thinkers that have extrapolated concise outcomes from their personal lives, called quotes. Quotes rooted in motivation psychology and articulated in practical terms can enhance daily living. The premise of the book, entitled, *Thoughts for Your Day*, is predicated on a simple rationale: the cultivation of a specific outcome and a pragmatic approach to integrating the information in the book into your life.

The simple rationale embraces the idea that thoughts serve as precursors to our actions and ultimately to our destinies. The term thought is defined as an idea or opinion produced by thinking. It was Ralph Waldo Emerson who said, "Sow a thought and you reap an action; sow an act and you reap a habit; sow a habit and you reap a character; sow a character and you reap a destiny." Did you notice the progression: thought, action, habit, character, and then destiny? In essence, changing your thoughts will empower you to change your life. Thoughts serve as fuel for the acquisition of your destiny. The idea is for you to soak your intellect daily into the powerful inspirational information contained in this book.

The cultivation of a specific outcome embraces the idea that a person can change their life through conscious endeavor. King Solomon provides his readers with important information in Proverbs 23:7 (KJV): "For as he thinketh in his heart, so is he." James Allen said succinctly, "Dream lofty dreams, and as you dream, so shall you become. Your vision is the promise of what you shall one day be; your ideal is the prophecy of what you shall at last unveil"

The practical approach lays out a systematic approach to the information contained in *Thoughts for Your Day*. This book is divided into eight themes, supported by forty concise writings that address specific issues germane to each theme.

The design of the book is communicated in the following subsections:

- New Feature: The Thought Knowledge College
- A Forty-Day Change Experience
- A scripture or quote reference that support the individual writing
- A positive message
- A call to action
- Meditating on a New Thought exercise
- Three-Step Information Integration Tool
- Expanded index to include quotes, principles, and scripture references

The Thought Knowledge College

The Thought Knowledge College is predicated on the realization that *thoughts* are ideas or opinions produced by thinking; *knowledge* is facts, information, and skills acquired by a person through experience or education; while a *college* can be expressed as a center for learning. In essence, the Thought Knowledge College represents an economy of thought expressed in principles starting with Genesis, a New Beginning. Meditations, Food for Contemplation, continues the journey of changing one's life through possibility thinking, articulated in the Thoughts for Your Day Brand.

Forty-Day Change Experience

Why the forty-day period? That's a good question. In surveying the biblical text, there are three specific forty-day change experiences that God used to transform a nation, transform a person, and initiate a ministry. God used a forty-day fast to transform the nation of Israel through Moses on the mountain. Elijah was transformed because he heard God's voice after forty days of fasting. God initiated the public ministry of Jesus by subjected him to forty days of fasting in the wilderness and then sent him forth with power.

A Scripture or Quote Reference

The scripture references serve as a spiritual compass that provides guidance and inspiration to the spiritual dimension of the human personality. The quote reference serves as a motivational compass designed to provide guidance and inspiration to the soul of the human personality. In Matthew 6:33, Jesus reminds us to seek first the kingdom of God and his righteousness. Moreover, King Solomon provides his readers with important wisdom in Proverbs 3:5–6 (NIV): "Trust in the LORD with all your heart and lean not on your own understanding; in all your ways submit to him, and he will make your paths straight."

A Positive Message

The necessity of filling your mind with positive information cannot be underestimated. It was the great motivational speaker Earl Nightingale that advocated the concept that we become what we think about all day long. The positive information is designed to orient your mentality each day toward thoughts that uplift and empower you in a sea of negative messages.

A Call to Action

It was Archimedes who said, "Give me a place to stand on, and I will move the Earth." The place to stand on is your day, and your goal is to move your world by enhancing your thought life for ten minutes each day. Indeed, man may design a spaceship that can break the earth's atmosphere and fly to the moon. Yet, no person has ever been able to break the atmosphere of self-imposed limitations without conscious endeavor. Finally, each writing contains a call to action, predicated on making a firm decision. The term *decide* is a Latin word that means to "cut off all other alternatives." We can either be held as prisoners of our thoughts, or they can liberate us.

Meditating on a New Thought Exercise

The Meditating on a New Thought exercise is predicated on three thought-provoking elements designed to facilitate critical thinking. The *Reflection Thought* extrapolates a precise thought from the current reading. The *Principle to Remember* focuses on a fundamental truth that supports the cultivation of an empowering thought life. And lastly, the *Question to Explore* is designed to elicit a subjective response from the very essence of who you are in the form of a journal response.

Three-Step Information Integration Tool

The Information Integration Tool is designed to help you integrate new information into your thought life with the outcome of living the Thoughts for Your Day Brand.

Expanded Index to include Quotes, Principles, and Scripture References

The expanded index to include quotes, principles, and scripture references is a resource designed to put these key elements at your fingertips. Les Brown, the great motivational speaker, once divulged that when he first started learning to speak professionally, he would memorize quotes and other important information. Doing this empowered him to become a walking library, with the ability to articulate the information he had memorized whenever he needed.

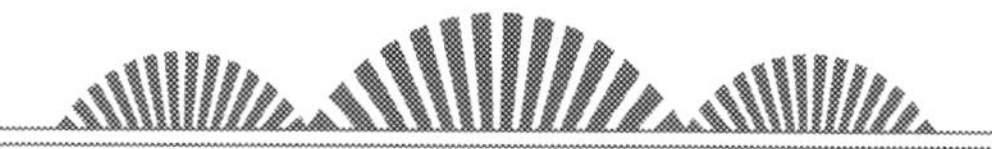

Theme 1

Self-Actualization

Day 1

Effective Decision-Making

Helen Keller said, "Life is short. Eat your dessert first!" Most mothers would not repeat this advice to their young children, but it does provide us with sage wisdom related to effective decision-making.

The word *decision* is from Latin, meaning to "cut off all other alternatives." The concept of effective decision-making is illustrated by Hernando Cortez in 1519 during the Spanish conquest of the Aztec empire. As the story goes, Cortez told his army to "burn the boats," which meant they would either conquer the territory and come back alive on somebody else's boats or they would die trying. Cortez made a firm decision to move forward in the realization of his goal at all costs. Effective decision-making is a lot like that!

Getting back to the advice that Helen Keller conveyed, we find this simple point: life is very uncertain. While some opportunities may repeat themselves over time, other opportunities only come once in a lifetime, so you must seize the moment. In Greek culture, there is a strange-looking statue called the "Opportunity Statue." It depicts a person's head with hair on one side and a smooth surface on the other side. It is taught that when the side of the head with hair passes in front of you, that is your opportunity to grab the hair and hold on it. Once the statue passes and you encounter the smooth surface of the head, you can no longer grab the hair, and your opportunity has passed you by.

Decide today to take hold of the opportunities that are in front of you. Once they are gone, they may be gone forever! Spend ten minutes listing your current opportunities for the purpose of taking action on the ones you will select. Decide to embrace effective decision-making. Think about it.

Day 1
Meditating on a New Thought Exercise

Reflection Thought: Making the most of every opportunity is a great way to live a life both on purpose and for a purpose.

Principle to Remember: While some opportunities may reappear over time, other opportunities only come once in a lifetime, so we must seize the moment.

Question to Explore: What opportunities do you have that are available for you to take hold of in your life today?

____

____

____

Day 2

Right Actions

In his Nobel Peace Prize acceptance speech on December 10, 1964, Martin Luther King Jr. said, "I believe that unarmed truth and unconditional love will have the final word in reality. That is why right, temporarily defeated, is stronger than evil triumphant."

Sometimes, it is easy to wonder whether one person can make a difference. It seems that we live in a world that prominently displays images and sound bites of evil dominating the social consciousness. For example, consider what is depicted on nightly news channels across the world. Don't fall into the trap of believing that your right action, expressed in love every day, fails to make a difference. You matter, and so does every right thing you do. Consider the mother who ensures that her children are fed while she goes to bed hungry. Consider the teacher or coach who inspired you to believe in yourself when no one else did. Ultimately, think about Jesus Christ dying on the cross, alone, with the sins of all humanity to bear. In each case, the action of an individual mattered, and so do your actions.

Spend ten minutes today contemplating and developing a list of people who have affected your life with right actions. Pick up the phone and let them know about the difference they made in your life. Decide to embrace right actions! Think about it!

Day 2
Meditating on a New Thought Exercise

Reflection Thought: Making the most of every opportunity is a great way to live a life both on purpose and for a purpose.

Principle to Remember: You matter, and so does every right thing you do!

Question to Explore: What is one right action that you need to make today?

____

____

____

Day 3

Defining Your Voice

King Solomon said in Proverbs 20:5 (NIV), "The purposes of a person's heart are deep waters, but one who has insight draws them out." A fish placed on dry land will die in a matter of minutes. When placed in water, that same fish swims with precision and skill.

Finding your voice in a world consisting of more than seven billion people is a lot like that. The term *voice* is defined as an "expression of opinion or desire." I believe that you come into this world programmed with greatness. However, finding your voice requires both precision and skill. Some environments are detrimental to achieving what Abraham Maslow articulated as self-actualization in his hierarchy-of-needs pyramid. Wrong people, geographical locations, and negativity represent dry ground for many of us. And like the fish that was unable to express its greatness, we find ourselves in a similar predicament.

On the other hand, when we encounter the right people, geographical locations, and individuals who build us up with positive energy, our true greatness has the capacity to be released.

Lastly, insight is defined as the ability to see clearly or to have a clear perception of reality. Take a moment to look into a mirror and notice the reflection. It's you! You were created with greatness built into the fabric of your intrinsic essence. Make a commitment at this moment never to compare yourself to anyone else ever again. The world does not need another Michael Jordan, Tiger Woods, or Whitney Houston. We simply need the greatness that has been placed into your heart.

Spend ten minutes today thanking God for the talents, abilities, and greatness he has placed inside you. Decide to embrace defining your voice. Think about it!

Day 3

Meditating on a New Thought Exercise

Reflection Thought: The moment you compare yourself to someone else is the moment you forfeit the greatness that is within you.

Principle to Remember: You were created with greatness built into the fabric of your intrinsic essence.

Question to Explore: What talents and qualities do you have that make you unique?

____

____

____

Day 4

The Element of Contrast in the Goal-Setting Process

King Solomon said in Proverbs 21:5 (KJV), "The plans of the diligent lead to profit as surely as haste leads to poverty." King Solomon provides a solid plan for achieving goals by utilizing the element of contrast in the goal-setting process.

As we approach the text, there are five areas that constitute the element of contrast. The first area deals with planning. Planning, consisting of detailed proposals for achieving a goal, is vital in your quest to achieve destiny acquisition. Without plans, goals tend to be abstract and futuristic in nature. The moment you capture the essence of your goals by writing them down is the moment they begin to become real. I'm reminded of a saying: "People don't plan to fail; they fail because they don't plan."

The second area focuses on diligence. Diligence means showing care and conscientiousness in one's work or duties. The actualization of your goals will tend to be realized in various stages of their development. For instance, in the initiation stage, you simply write the goal down. It is at that point that the real journey begins. Diligence requires steady perseverance, often in the face of many roadblocks and setbacks.

The third area examines the outcome of producing profit as a result of conscientious endeavor. Profit can be defined as financial gain or the production of something. I believe that profit transcends the traditional definition of obtaining money. When we are engaged in worthwhile activities that contribute to the good of society, we better our own lives. Therefore, we profit from the satisfaction of knowing we help others.

At this point, King Solomon shifts from the positive aspects of planning to the detrimental components of haste and poverty. Haste is the fourth area that Solomon addresses, and in this context, it means "movement characterized by excessive speed or urgency." As we consider the current societal context endemic in American culture, haste rules the day. Multitasking has become the norm for many of us, causing effective planning to become secondary. We simply live from one moment to the next.

The final point that Solomon addresses is the idea of poverty. Poverty is a term that means a "state of being extremely poor or destitute." Operating from a perspective of haste causes one to miss out on many of the great treasures of life. Some of us are so busy walking hastily around the rose garden of life that we fail to stop and smell the roses. Roses can represent spending precious time with the family, working on our talents, or building a healthy body. At the end of the day, poverty is often the result of failed planning and hasty living.

Spend ten minutes today planning and enjoying the roses of your life for the purpose of realizing your goals. Decide to embrace the element of contrast in the goal-setting process. Think about it!

Day 4
Meditating on a New Thought Exercise

Reflection Thought: God provides us with beautiful treasures each day simply as gifts from his heart. Gifts like watching the sun rise or holding hands with someone you love are free for the taking. The key is to slow down enough to appreciate those gifts!

Principle to Remember: Some of us are so busy walking hastily around the rose garden of life that we fail to stop and smell the roses.

Question to Explore: As you examine your current reality, what roses has God placed in your life to enjoy?

____

____

____

Day 5

Three Realities of Goals

Earl Nightingale said, "People with goals succeed because they know where they're going." As a kid, I remember looking into the darkness and observing the effervescent light displays perpetuated by lightning bugs meandering through the night. I remember being captivated by the spectacular displays of bright light as the bugs became aerial artists.

Goals are like the bright lights that contrasted against the darkness that held the horizon captive. In the quote referenced above, Earl Nightingale quickly divides the world into two types of people: people who set goals and people who do not set goals. As you consider the two types of individuals, what type do you consider yourself to be? That is the question we must all answer. As we consider the words of Earl Nightingale, there are three points worthy of discussion. Goals help you to succeed. The term succeed means to "achieve an aim or result." Defining goals for your life gives you worthy objectives to strive toward every single day. A person without goals is like a map without detail: both will lead you to nowhere. Goals ensure that you have a destination to aim for. Without them, you are likely to simply exist. Goals provide a direction for your life. Imagine getting into your car without a destination in mind. Eventually, you would run out of gas just blindly driving around. Sadly, many individuals wake up every day without a destination in mind, only to find themselves shipwrecked on an island called mediocrity. Goals provide a destination for your journey and ensure that you use your resources wisely. Goals let you know when you have achieved your desired outcome. I love the period that goes at the end of each sentence. The period marks the completion of a series of words that convey thought and meaning. The period also indicates the time when you can move on to the next sentence. In very much the same way, our lives should represent a continuous flow of achieving a goal and then moving on to the next one.

Spend ten minutes today defining your goals for the purpose of pursuing them every day until they are accomplished. Decide to embrace three realities of goals. Think about it!

Day 5
Meditating on a New Thought Exercise

Reflection Thought: A worthy goal is likely to add years to your life and life to your years!

Principle to Remember: A person without goals is like a map without detail: both will lead you to nowhere.

Question to Explore: Are you living life with concrete goals?

___

___

___

THEME 2

The Power of Friendship

Day 6

Choosing Wise Friends

King Solomon said in Proverbs 13:20 (NIV), "He who walks with the wise grows wise, but a companion of fools suffers harms." If you were to turn on the news on any given night, you would find many examples of individuals who choose to associate with peers who would not be considered wise. From a Christian perspective, a person is wise when he fears and respects God. Notice what Solomon says in Proverbs 9:10 (NIV): "The fear of the LORD is the beginning of wisdom, and knowledge of the Holy One is understanding."

Wisdom, or the quality of having experience, knowledge, and good judgment, is a prerequisite for living a complete life. As we consider the theme of friendship, perhaps there is no other source of influence in our lives, apart from our relationship with our family members. Please hear me clearly: "You are affected by the people you consider friends." The reality of learning vicariously through others is eloquently communicated in the social learning theory, developed by Albert Bandura in the 1960s. The Bobo doll experiments featured a child-sized inflatable doll with a weighted bottom that caused it to pop back up after being knocked down. Small children who witnessed adults behaving aggressively toward the doll emulated the same behaviors when allowed to play with the doll independently, a dynamic Bandura referred to as *vicarious reinforcement*. In short, the small children learned by observation.

In the last analysis, asking for God to give you the wisdom to select wise friends is one of the greatest things you can do to ensure your success. The prison system is filled with individuals serving life sentences because they were guilty by association, which the legal system refers to as conspiracy.

Spend ten minutes considering the importance of choosing wise friends, and then ask God to give you the wisdom to fill your life with quality individuals with highly developed personalities. Decide today to embrace choosing wise friends. Think about it!

Day 6
Meditating on a New Thought Exercise

Reflection Thought: The friends that you invite into your life influence you either negatively or positively. A wise person chooses friends who take them to new horizons!

Principle to Remember: As you consider the importance of choosing wise friends, ask God to give you the wisdom to fill your life with quality individuals with highly developed personalities.

Question to Explore: What type of friends make up your current social circle? Are they helping you realize your destiny or preventing you from realizing your destiny?

____

____

____

Day 7

Experiencing the Special Place

Marc Roberts said, "Friendship is a duality in motion, it is both spiritual and geographical simultaneously." The human condition is filled with uncertainty. The one actuality that remains certain, in all generations, is that we were created for relationships with others. The developmental process for all human beings is expressed in three stages: dependence, independence, and interdependence. At each stage, the essence of the *special place* is made known. I define the special place as a spiritual and geographical reality between two people. This friendship or close relationship between individuals has a spiritual component. The spiritual component is depicted by continuity, as if two hearts beat as one. Certain people who enter our lives possess this quality of friendship, and we are so much better because of them. The geographical component is simply the temporal reality of a place that contains the two. In other words, wherever the two hearts are in the space-time continuum, the friendship thrives. Lastly, as we consider the concept of the special place in friendship relationships, we must consider Maslow's hierarchy of needs. According to Abraham Maslow, love and belonging are essential ingredients in the quest for self-actualization, or becoming the very best that you can become. Friendships, family, and sexual intimacy compose the level of Maslow's pyramid relating to love and belonging. Without the nurturing environment of friendships, which I refer to as the special place, it is extremely difficult to become the best person you were created to become.

Spend ten minutes today connecting with a friend who has meant a lot to you over the years. Express to them in words their true value in your life. Decide today to embrace the special place. Think about it!

Day 7
Meditating on a New Thought Exercise

Reflection Thought: A true friendship is not so much about what you can get out of the relationship but rather what you can give to the relationship.

Principle to Remember: Certain people who enter our lives possess the quality of friendship, and we are so much better because of them.

Question to Explore: What are you giving in your current relationship to enhance the lives of those you call friends?

____

____

____

Day 8

The Power of Friendship

Samuel the seer provides us with important information related to the friendship of Jonathan and David in 1 Samuel 18:1 (ESV): "As soon as he had finished speaking to Saul, the soul of Jonathan was knit to the soul of David, and Jonathan loved him as his own soul." In many writings, the soul has been described as the part of the human being that houses the mind, will, intellect, and personality. The term knit is defined as the "uniting or interlocking of items together." As we consider this idea of two souls becoming one in the friendship of Jonathan and David, we literally see the mind, will, intellect, and personality of the two joined in an eternal bond. In everyday life, this resembled Jonathan and David wishing the very best upon one another. It meant that they felt each other's pain and shared their visions for the future, while helping each other meander through the difficult issues of life. Ultimately, Jonathan was responsible for helping David ascend to the throne of Israel, where he reigned for forty years. As we consider the anatomy of the friendship that existed between Jonathan and David, a couple of points stand out. Firstly, true friendship is solidified in a bond that knits together the souls of individuals. Secondly, the friendship bond is designed as a tool to help individuals navigate the vicissitudes of life. Lastly, true friendship has an eternal component that transcends the natural and is really supernatural, because two hearts find the rhythm of life and beat as one.

Spend ten minutes thanking God for the friends he has bought into your life, in addition to thanking him in advance for the friends who will eventually come into your life. Decide today to understand the power of friendship. Think about it!

Day 8
Meditating on a New Thought Exercise

Reflection Thought: A true friend desires the very best for your life.

Principle to Remember: True friendship has an eternal component that transcends the natural and is really supernatural, because two hearts find the rhythm of life and beat as one.

Question to Explore: Are you the type of friend who adds value to your cherished friendships?

___

___

___

Day 9

The True Cost of Friendship

Aristotle said, "The antidote for fifty enemies is one friend." Perhaps you don't have fifty enemies, but the message in the quote denotes the importance of defining your true friends. The term friend is defined as a "person that you have a bond of mutual affection with, typically exclusive of sexual or family relations." As you consider your current reality, how many of your current friends truly fit that description? The simple and obvious point I am making is this: friendship comes with a price. Let's examine a concise dynamic of friendship. that will help you determine the price associated with true friendship. According to Proverbs 18:24 (NIV), "One who has unreliable friends soon comes to ruin, but there is a friend who sticks closer than a brother." A price associated with friendship is reliability or to be consistently good in quality or performance. Consider a brother; we typically think of someone who will be there through thick and thin. There is nothing worse than being deserted by individuals you thought were your friends during times of crisis. Many people mistake associations with individuals they encounter regularly with friendship; however, this assumption evolves into a real crisis when assumed friends are nowhere to be found on the day of trouble. These same individuals arrive early to cookouts on your dime and favors performed on your time. As you access your friendship list today, it may be necessary to cultivate a relationship audit. Deleting assumed friends from your psychological capacity is a lot like deleting friends from Facebook. You still speak and smile when you see them, but they no longer have access to your important information.

Spend ten minutes making a list of friends that you will keep and associates you plan to delete. Decide today to embrace the true cost of friendship. Think about it!

Day 9
Meditating on a New Thought Exercise

Reflection Thought: One friend that sticks with you through good and bad times is worth more than a million dollars in the bank. A sad situation is when a person learns to make money but not friends and dies a lonely death.

Principle to Remember: Deleting assumed friends from your psychological capacity is a lot like deleting friends from Facebook. You still speak and smile when you see them, but they no longer have access to your important information.

Question to Explore: Is there a price to pay for cultivating effective friendships?

____
____
____

Day 10

Understanding the Power of the Emotional Bank Account

An unknown author said, "Friendship isn't a big thing; it's a million little things." This quote captures the essence of the friendship experience. Understanding the analogy of the *emotional bank account* is key to developing great friendships, by explicitly addressing the cumulative aspect of the relationship. The cumulative (increasing in quantity by successive additions) dynamic of friendships reinforces the idea of an emotional bank account. Many of us use bank accounts as safe places to store our money. The more deposits we make into the bank account, the more the account grows in worth as a result of interest and new money we place in the account. In very much the same way, we can liken the heart of our friend to an emotional bank account. The more deposits we make over time, the more valuable the relationship becomes. Communication is the key to understanding what constitutes a deposit for the person you are in a friendship with. For instance, one of your friends may like a nice card for their birthday, while another friend would prefer you taking them out to dinner. As we learn what a deposit looks like in our cherished friendships, we can be strategic in making deposits.

I must mention that withdrawals can occur as well. Just as the money decreases in our bank accounts due to repeated withdrawals, the same holds true in our friendships. If your friend values confidentiality but learns you have exposed details about something, they confided in you about, you, in essence, have made a withdrawal from the emotional bank account that you have with that person. The idea of the emotional bank account can be applied to any relationship, primarily because we are dealing with matters of the heart.

Spend ten minutes today thinking about ways you can make a deposit in your most cherished friendships. If you have made a withdrawal in the past, perhaps the best way to make a great deposit is to simply say the magic words, "I am sorry." Decide today to embrace understanding the power of the emotional bank account. Think about it!

Day 10
Meditating on a New Thought Exercise

Reflection Thought: A friendship is a constant exchange of therapeutic energy that improves the lives of the people in the friendship.

Principle to Remember: Communication is key in understanding what constitutes a deposit for the person you are in a friendship with.

Question to Explore: Do your current friendships leave you with energy for days or depleted and frustrated for weeks?

____

____

____

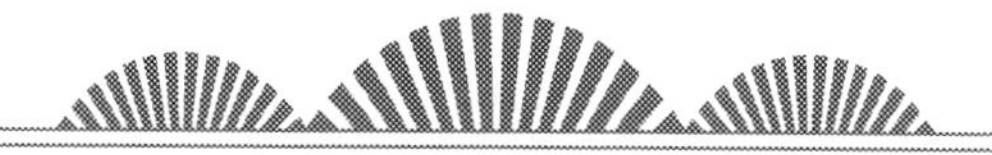

Theme 3

Goal Setting

Day 11

Releasing Your True Self through the Power of Goal Setting

T. S. Eliot said, "Only those who will risk going too far can possibly find out how far one can go." Baby eagles are forced to learn to fly. The mother eagle instinctively deconstructs her nest when her babies reach a certain stage in their developmental process. What once was a comfortable nursery suddenly becomes an uncomfortable temporary holding cell. The mother literally forces her young babies into their eventual destiny. In essence, she is making the statement to them that conveys you were created to fly, so do it! Everything you need to be successful is programmed into the essence of who you are. And so, one by one, the little eagles transition from the safety of the nest to the peril of the unknown. As the rapid descent elicits and makes a demand on the greatness contained within them, one by one, each little eagle spreads their wings and begin to soar as they were intended to.

As you set goals for your life, you will meander from the safety of the known into the wilderness of the unknown. It is our struggles that unlock the greatness that was placed in our hearts before we ever breathed our first breath. How far can you possibly go? Are you willing to pay the price to unlock the greatness within? Make a decision to soar as you were intended by setting demanding goals and entering into the unknown. It is only then that the true self is released.

Spend ten minutes developing a list of challenging goals for the purpose of making a demand on your greatness. Decide to release your true self through the power of goal setting. Think about it!

Day 11
Meditating on a New Thought Exercise

Reflection Thought: Our struggles unlock the greatness placed in our hearts before we ever breathed our first breath.

Principle to Remember: Everything you need to be successful is programmed into the essence of who you are.

Question to Explore: What goals do you need to set to release the greatness that resides inside of you?

___

___

___

Day 12

The Power of Goals

Les Brown said, "Shoot for the moon. Even if you miss, you'll land among the stars." The problem for most of us is that we don't shoot at all and we hit! Low goals are a slam dunk! Mediocrity is the norm of our day. Consider the following story, which has been a part of motivational psychology for years. An experiment was done involving graduates from Yale University in the 1940s. In that graduating class, 3 percent of the graduates wrote down their financial goals for life after graduation. When they had their twenty-year class reunion, it was found that the 3 percent that wrote down their goals had accumulated more wealth than the other 97 percent of the class that had not written down their goals. I find this to be an amazing testament to the power of goal setting. In closing, if you fail to plan then, in essence, you are planning to fail.

Goals that are expressed using the SMART acronym are best. Goals need to be *smart*, *measurable*, *attainable*, *realistic*, and *timely*.

Spend ten minutes writing out a list of smart goals for the purpose of becoming a better goal setter! Decide today to embrace the power of goals. Think about it!

Day 12
Meditating on a New Thought Exercise

Reflection Thought: In life, if you fail to plan, you are planning to fail.

Principle to Remember: The problem for most of us is that we don't shoot at all and we hit! Low goals are a slam dunk!

Question to Explore: What five goals can you write down on paper and progress in the next three months?

____

____

____

Day 13

The Power of Written Goals

The prophet Habakkuk said in Habakkuk 2:2 (EAS): "And the LORD answered me: 'Write the vision; make it plain on tablets, so he may run who reads it.'" As we consider the anatomy of goal setting, writing your goals down clearly is an important step. Many people dislike Apple products, but did you know you actually have an "apple" computer even though you may have never actually purchased one? In the back of your head, at the base of your skull, is a bundle of nerves about the size of an apple, called the reticular activating system (RAS). The reticular activating system has many different functions; however, I only want to accentuate one. The ability of the RAS to screen out unnecessary stimuli and information plays an important role in the goal-setting process. Let me explain. Have you ever purchased a specific make and model automobile, such as a Toyota Camry? Prior to getting that automobile, you probably did not notice other people driving them as you processed the events of your day. After purchasing your Camry, you notice them all over the place. Because of your financial investment, the reticular activating system hones in like a global positioning system, prompting your conscious mind to pay attention. When you write your goal down, you are enlisting both your conscious and unconscious mind to pay attention and focus on your goal, thus harnessing the power of concentration. Suddenly, your abstract vision is distilled into concrete missiles of concentration designed to obliterate your clearly defined target goals.

Spend ten minutes today writing down several of your goals that apply to specific areas. State your goals using "I …" statements. For instance, "I will spend thirty minutes on the elliptical machine at the gym today." In the words of *GI Joe*, "Now you know, and knowing is half the battle." The other half is to make your goal a reality through positive action! Decide to embrace the power of written goals. Think about it!

Day 13
Meditating on a New Thought Exercise

Reflection Thought: Abstract ideas become concrete goals when you take the time to write them down.

Principle to Remember: When you write your goal down, you are enlisting both your conscious and unconscious mind to pay attention and focus in on your goals, thus harnessing the power of concentration.

Question to Explore: Where do you see yourself in five years? If you cannot answer that question in concrete terms, chances are you will end up where life takes you.

____

____

____

Day 14

Utilizing Perseverance and Visualization as Tools for Accomplishing Your Goal

The apostle Paul said in Philippians 3:14 (NIV), "I press on toward the goal to win the prize for which God has called me heavenward in Christ Jesus." The term goal is defined as the "object of a person's ambition or effort." For the apostle Paul, it was to preach the Gospel to the Gentiles. As we consider Paul's efforts toward the realization of his life's purpose, we can extrapolate several insights from the text as an educational moment. Your goal will require you to press toward a higher calling. To press means to "apply force or pressure." For our purpose, we will equate pressure to perseverance or steadfastness in doing something despite difficulty. This dynamic is seen whenever NASA commissions a space shuttle to the moon. The majority of the force and energy is expended during the first few minutes of liftoff. Once the space shuttle pierces the earth's atmosphere, less fuel and force are needed to continue the mission. As you consider your goal, you must apply tremendous pressure to break out of ineffective atmospheres—habits and propensities that you have maintained up to the point where you have decided to change.

The second point that Paul teaches is that our goal is actually a prize. The term prize is defined as a "thing given as a reward." This is important! If your goal is to earn a degree, project yourself into the future, walking across the stage with your degree in the presence of loved ones who are giving you the highest applause. Between the time you decide to earn your degree and the time you walk across the stage, there will be difficult days. The vision you hold in your heart of the final outcome will serve as fuel to propel you through those tough days. Paul experienced beatings, shipwrecks, and imprisonments, yet he persevered during tough days to become the most prolific writer in the New Testament, writing thirteen of the twenty-seven books that comprise the text. Make it a point to press toward the goals that you have written down and cultivated into desired outcomes.

Spend ten minutes thinking about what the full realization of your goal will feel like; do this many times throughout your day, until the day comes when it becomes a reality. Decide to embrace utilizing perseverance and visualization as tools for accomplishing your goal. Think about it!

Day 14
Meditating on a New Thought Exercise

Reflection Thought: As you seek to accomplish the goals you set for your life, you will experience both difficulty and success. The wise person is the one who anticipates both!

Principle to Remember: The vision you hold in your heart of the final outcome will serve as fuel to propel you through those tough days.

Question to Explore: What is a goal that you would like to achieve? What will it feel like when you accomplish that goal?

____

____

____

Day 15

Paying the Cost for Achieving Your Goals

Sidney Howard said, "Half of knowing what you want is knowing what you must give up before you get it." As you enter into the world of goal setting, you will be forced to make some very clear decisions. When you determine what you want in life and write it down as a goal, you will be forced to say yes to some things and no to others. Did you know that research has been conducted on the power of associations and friendships? On average, a person will make within two to three thousand dollars more or less than their three closest friends. It was found that hanging around obese or overweight friends greatly increases your potential to become obese or overweight yourself. Les Brown, the great motivational speaker refers to this dynamic as a *mind virus*. As you examine your life and the goals that you have set, you must now determine what you must give up to get them. Often, the list is replete with time-wasting activities and includes ending bad relationships and negative habits and adopting a new propensity to develop your potential.

Spend ten minutes today clarifying and writing down your goals. After you write them down, decide what you must give up to achieve your intended outcome. The last step is to resolve to carry out your plan using positive action. Decide today to embrace paying the cost for achieving your goals. Think about it!

Day 15
Meditating on a New Thought Exercise

Reflection Thought: The quality of your goals to a large extent determines the quality of your life.

Principle to Remember: When you determine what you want in life and write it down as a goal, you will be forced to say yes to some things and no to other things.

Question to Explore: What are the things you must say no to in order to say yes to the goals you want to achieve in life.

____
____
____

THEME 4

Random Thoughts

Day 16

Three Sentiments of Legacy Cultivation

In 2 Kings 13:21 (NIV), we find these words: "Once while some Israelites were burying a man, suddenly they saw a band of raiders; so, they threw the man's body into Elisha's tomb. When the body touched Elisha's bones, the man came to life and stood up on his feet." The essence of legacy cultivation is contained in the anatomy of this powerful scripture reference. I define legacy cultivation as the endowment we leave that empowers future generations to stand to their feet as a result of becoming the individuals they were created to become. As we approach the text, there are three sentiments that the writer presents. The first sentiment reveals that the young man was dead and void of life. In our society today, it is not uncommon to meet men and women that are physically alive but dead in relation to the tremendous gift of greatness that resides within them. Their greatest need is to experience new life. The second sentiment discloses that circumstances caused the Israelites to abandon their strategy of simply burying the young man, by abruptly throwing the corpse into the tomb with Elisha. The term circumstance is defined as "fact or condition connected with an event or action." Your conception and subsequent birth serves as the impetus for meeting the great minds contained in the past and present. Elisha's legacy was replete with examples of the greatness he expressed during his life experience. His bones represented a body or an endowment of life-giving vitality that could energize future generations even after he experienced physical mortality. As you consider your own legacy, what will you leave behind? The third sentiment imparts that the young man came to life after he experienced the residue of Elisha's bones. This was indicated by the dead man standing to his feet. Every book, poem, or business that you develop as a result of your life has the potential to cause future generations to stand to their feet. A person does not have to be physically dead to be dead in relation to their destiny. Every day, men and women meander into eternity clothed with the garments of obscurity. Their obituary reads, "He was born, she paid her taxes, and he died." On her deathbed, the books, poems, and works of art she was designed to create surrounded her in anger. They simply wanted to know why she failed to give birth to them so that future generations might enjoy their beauty. Lastly, they are angry because they were never set free to free others!

Spend ten minutes writing down goals to accomplish as a result of your life experience to empower future generations. Decide today to embrace three sentiments of legacy cultivation. Think about it!

Day 16
Meditating on a New Thought Exercise

Reflection Thought: The world is waiting on you to tap into your greatness. We will celebrate with you as you become the best version of yourself!

Principle to Remember: A person does not have to be physically dead to be dead in relation to their destiny.

Question to Explore: What is the legacy that you will leave behind after you experience physical mortality?

____

____

____

DAY 17

The Principle of Submission

Jesus Christ said in Luke 22:42 (KJV), "Father, if you are willing, take this cup from me; yet not my will, but yours be done." As we explore the theme of effectiveness, it is important to develop a clear definition of the term. Effectiveness is the degree to which something is successful in producing a desired result. The life of Jesus Christ represents the actualization of a successful outcome. In the field of systematic theology, we refer to the person and work of Jesus Christ as Christology. The word "Christology" comes from two Greek words, meaning "Christ/Messiah" and "word," which combine to mean the "study of Christ." By the time we approach Luke 22:42, Dr. Luke points us toward one of the primary facets relating to the life of Jesus Christ. He was born to die, and yet the realization of that actuality produced tears that resembled blood drops on that night of purposeful prayer in the Garden of Gethsemane. Jesus revealed the agony of his purpose by committing to the principle of submission. While many rely on their own strength and skill to produce an outcome, Jesus relied on the strength of his father to fulfill his destiny. I feel wholeheartedly that there is a lesson for you and me to learn as we navigate our experience here on earth. The surrender of our will to the higher calling that God has for us comes at a price. Like Christ, we may find ourselves up early in the morning, in isolation, asking God to give us the strength to commit to his purpose in our lives. Like Christ, we may cry tears that reflect the struggle in the subterranean depths of our souls. And like Christ, we too can experience the peace that accompanies a will that submits fully to the will or our Heavenly Father.

Spend ten minutes today in meaningful prayer for the purpose of seeking God to obtain his strength in empowering you to submit fully to his will in your life. Decide today to embrace the principle of submission.

Day 17
Meditating on a New Thought Exercise

Reflection Thought: A life well lived is a life that is given in service while one lives.

Principle to Remember: While many rely on their own strength and skill to produce an outcome, Jesus relied on the strength of his father to fulfill his destiny.

Question to Explore: What are you willing to die for? Until you can fully answer that question, you are not truly ready to live.

____

____

____

Day 18

The True Value of Exercise

The apostle Paul conveys in 1 Timothy 4:8 (NIV), "For physical training is of some value, but godliness has value for all things, holding promise for both the present life and the life to come." What is the true value of exercise? Perhaps one way to attack that question is to examine some data related to obesity and lack of physical activity. According to data aggregated by the Centers for Disease Control and Prevention, 35.7 percent of adults are considered obese. Health problems associated by obesity include heart disease, stroke, type 2 diabetes, and certain types of cancer, some leading to preventable death. The estimated annual medical cost of obesity in the US was $147 billion in 2008. The average cost of medical care for obese individuals contrasted to individuals that were at normal weight was $1,429 higher. In essence, I believe the true value of physical training (exercise) is that it helps us acquire our destiny by providing a number of measurable benefits. Some positive benefits of exercising include weight control and reduction of cardiovascular disease, type 2 diabetes, and some forms of cancer. Other benefits include strengthening your muscles and bones and improving mental health and mood. Studies even reveal that exercising increases your chances of living a longer life. The body was created for movement and totally regenerates all of its cells about every seven years. The next time you are feeling a little cranky, take a thirty-minute walk and listen to some uplifting music. Exercise is good for the soul!

Spend ten minutes today designing an exercise plan for your life and they do it! Decide to embrace the true value of exercise. Think about it!

Day 18
Meditating on a New Thought Exercise

Reflection Thought: A physically fit body is a good vehicle to the acquisition of your destiny.

Principle to Remember: The body was created for movement and totally regenerates all of its cells about every seven years.

Question to Explore: Do you view exercise as a chore or as a high-leverage activity that can add years to your life?

___

___

___

Day 19

A Perspective on Joy

Emily Dickinson said, "The mere sense of living is joy enough." It is a sad commentary that so many people seem to lack joy in life. In this concise quote, I believe that Emily helps us to understand the true definition of joy, simplify the experience of joy, and apply joy to the pragmatic aspects of daily living. The understanding of joy is absolutely critical in your quest to living a joyful existence. A concise definition of joy is simply this: joy is a feeling of great pleasure and happiness and is one of the great emotions endemic to the human condition. As we grow in our understanding of joy, we are in a better position to realize the many opportunities to experience joy in the precious moments that we are blessed with each day. Simplifying the experience of joy leads one to a joyful reality. A closer examination of the term "sense of living" has a profound lesson for all that would listen. Living is not just going through the mechanical or biological functions of the human body but rather is connecting joy to the simple things of life. Applying joy to the pragmatic aspects of daily living ensures a joyful existence. Joy is experienced by the mother that kisses her child goodnight. Joy is experienced by the father who holds his daughter close when she is afraid. Joy is walking outside and feeling the sunshine on your face in the midst of a hectic day. In essence, there is the potential to experience joy in every moment that we are blessed to realize the simple things of life. As we approach each moment with an attitude of gratitude, we unleash the spirit of humility. It is then that we embrace the idea that living is joy enough.

Spend ten minutes making a list of the things in life that bring you joy. Decide today to embrace a perspective on joy. Think about it!

Day 19
Meditating on a New Thought Exercise

Reflection Thought: The realization of joy in daily living has to do with embracing the blessings that you already have.

Principle to Remember: As we approach each moment with an attitude of gratitude, we unleash the spirit of humility.

Question to Explore: What are five things that bring you joy in the various areas of your life?

____

____

____

Day 20

Insanity Defined

Albert Einstein said, "Insanity: doing the same thing over and over again and expecting different results." It is easy to continue doing the things we are accustomed to doing. It's something about operating in a comfort zone that is appealing, since most people are creatures of habit. Yet, the people that changed the world refused to operate in comfort zones but continually embraced uncomfortable zones that pushed them into self-actualization. Today, we study them on the pages of history. This is precisely why we must examine our habits each day. Poor habits lead to poor results. Good habits lead to good results. For example, constantly spending more money than you make over a period of time can be disastrous and typically leads to debt. Paying yourself first and depositing a portion of that money into a savings account is a wealth-building habit. Both habits produce an outcome. One leads to poverty, while the other has the potential to lead to wealth. This simple perspective dealing with finances is just one of the many habits we must examine if we are currently experiencing insane results.

Spend ten minutes making a list of issues you must confront, in order to get off the insanity treadmill. Decide today to embrace *insanity defined.* Think about it!

Day 20
Meditating on a New Thought Exercise

Reflection Thought: The ability to effectively examine your life creates the ability to change your life.

Principle to Remember: It's something about operating in a comfort zone that is appealing, since most people are creatures of habit. Yet, the people that changed the world refused to operate in comfort zones but continually embraced uncomfortable zones that pushed them into self-actualization.

Question to Explore: What is one comfort zone that you know you need to break free of today?

____

____

____

THEME 5

Life Perspectives

Day 21

Making the Most of Spare Moments

Ralph Waldo Emerson said, "Guard well your spare moments. They are like uncut diamonds. Discard them and their value will never be known. Improve them and they will become the brightest gems in a useful life." The ability to manage spare moments will change your life. Most people have a dream or goal that they want to accomplish. The problem arises when they say they will get to that goal one day, when they have more time. One day never comes, and the book or song in their heart is never written. If you decide to connect your goal with a spare moment in each day, soon your goal will become a reality. Sayings like "Rome was not built in a day" and "the best way to eat an elephant is one bite at a time" contain real wisdom. Don't attempt to complete your goal all at once. Just work on it a little every day. Before long, your spare moments will produce the brightest gems for many to behold.

Spend ten minutes developing a list of goals you want to accomplish, and then work to accomplish them with the spare moments you have each day. Decide to embrace making the most of spare moments. Think about it!

Day 21

Meditating on a New Thought Exercise

Reflection Thought: As you examine your day, where can you find ten minutes to work on a goal that will improve the quality of your life.

Principle to Remember: The ability to manage spare moments will change your life.

Question to Explore: What is one goal that you have put off for years?

____

____

____

Day 22

Releasing Your True Value

Albert Einstein said, Try not to become a man of success, but rather try to become a man of value." When one attempts to define success based on the external world, the result is often confusion. Many people live their entire lives feeling like failures because they never live up to the expectations of their parents, teachers, and important members of a specific group. No matter how you examine an apple tree, the result will always be the same. It will remain an apple tree. The secret is to define your inner greatness. It is at that place that you find the power for living. You are here because the world needs what has been placed inside you. The more you can execute and operate out of the value that lies inside of you, the more harmonious your existence will be.

Spend ten minutes listing your talents on a piece of paper. There, you will find your true value to society. Decide today to embrace releasing your true value. Think about it!

Day 22
Meditating on a New Thought Exercise

Reflection Thought: Every person comes into the world with preloaded greatness and talents. Work is the vehicle to releasing that greatness into the world.

Principle to Remember: Many people live their entire lives feeling like failures because they never live up to the expectations of their parents, teachers, and important members of a specific group.

Question to Explore: Can you describe in words the value that lies inside you?

____

____

____

Day 23

Breaking Cycles

Martin Luther King said, "Returning violence for violence multiplies violence, adding deeper darkness to a night already devoid of stars. … Hate cannot drive out hate: only love can do that." It takes one person to break a cycle. You may be asking the question, "What are you referring too?" The late Steven Covey, the author of *The 7 Habits of Highly Effective People*, used the term "transition person" to accentuate the qualities of change, persistence, and fortitude of character to choose the different path. Robert Frost, in his poem, "The Road Not Taken," describes it as "the path that was less taken," and that made all the difference in the world for him.

So, let's extrapolate the previous sentences into cogent statements as they relate to love. Returning violence for violence has become the norm. An example of this is the road rage that we frequently hear about in the news. Choosing to love in the face of violence is character in motion. One person can break the cycle of hate on any given day by choosing to love instead of hate. Better yet, if you have been at odds with a parent, sibling, co-worker, etc., choose to be a transition person and break the cycle of hate, which is often expressed as non-communication. Pick up the phone and make that call today. Have that conversation. Let that person know that you love and care for them, because tomorrow is not promised. The Latin term *carpe diem* means "seize the day," which often is communicated as "seize the moment"!

Spend ten minutes proactively developing strategies to break negative cycles in your family, community, and society that you are passionate about! Decide to embrace breaking cycles. Think about it!

Day 23
Meditating on a New Thought Exercise

Reflection Thought: It takes one person choosing to operate in love to break a cycle of hate.

Principle to Remember: Choosing to love in the face of violence is character in motion.

Question to Explore: As you consider your life, what is one cycle that you can work to break today?

____

____

____

Day 24

Fifth-Generational Time Management, a New Paradigm That Promotes Effectiveness

Steven Covey said, "Start with the end in mind." Understanding Fifth-Generational Time Management, a New Paradigm That Promotes Effectiveness, is vital to your quest to becoming successful at causing intended results. Mr. Covey advocated starting with the end in mind as a prerequisite for proactive behavior. Some people spend a lifetime climbing up the ladder of success only to find that they have climbed up the wrong ladder when they get to the top. In my twenty-plus years of working in higher education, healthcare, and ministry, I have found that two important steps and one realization are important in the life-management process. Traditional time-management techniques taught individuals to manage and manipulate chronological units called years, months, weeks, days, hours, minutes, and seconds. The outcome over the years has distilled into individuals cramming more and more into an already busy schedule, leading some to aimless diversions.

Please meditate on this sentiment for a moment. On your deathbed, you are not going to wish you spent a few extra hours at the office; rather, you will wish you had spent time cultivating relationships with those you love. So how do we avoid climbing the wrong ladder of success? The first step involves defining your value system. A value (or something that is important to you) is a vehicle that ultimately leads you to your purpose.

The second step in the process involves the action of superimposing your value system onto your day. To superimpose means to place or lay one thing over another. This is important because often we find people and urgencies fully covering our day with their demands. When we superimpose our value system, we are living out of the mission and purpose components of our hearts. In everyday life, this might look like you valuing physical fitness and walking for thirty minutes. You make a predetermined decision to not let less important activities hijack your commitment. Lastly, we must all come to this realization as it relates to life. Each day becomes the medium of exchange between ingenuity and physical mortality. In short, the entrance into every new day places us closer to our final day. The full appreciation of this temporal quality of life becomes the impetus for helping us make the most of each day we are blessed with.

Spend ten minutes today designing your value system and then superimposing your values onto your day. Decide today to embrace "Fifth-Generational Time Management, a New Paradigm That Promotes Effectiveness." Think about it!

Day 24
Meditating on a New Thought Exercise

Reflection Thought: Some people spend a lifetime climbing up the ladder of success only to find that they have climbed up the wrong ladder when they get to the top.

Principle to Remember: On your deathbed, you are not going to wish you had spent a few extra hours at the office! You will probably wish you had spent more hours cultivating relationships with those you love.

Question to Explore: As you think about your life, what are your most important relationships, and what's one thing you can do today to improve them?

____

____

____

DAY 25

Prayer—the Essential Ingredient in Lifestyle Design

The apostle James said in James 5:16 (NIV), "Therefore confess your sins to each other and pray for each other so that you may be healed. The prayer of a righteous person is powerful and effective." Prayer is an essential ingredient in the process of lifestyle design. There are five guidelines that James provides for his readers in this scripture reference.

- **Guideline 1.** It is important to confess our sins to one another. God never designed his Church to function in isolation. He intended for individuals to experience life as a corporate community, navigating the mountaintop and valley experiences together. Confession is a great virtue to develop.
- **Guideline 2.** It is important to pray for one another. Prayer is a solemn request for help or an expression of thanks addressed to God. As we hear about the confessed sins of our brothers and sisters, it is our job to seek the one from where our help comes from on their behalf. The Psalmist conveys in Psalm 121:2 (NIV), "My help comes from the LORD, the Maker of heaven and earth."
- **Guideline 3.** The righteous person becomes righteous based on the person and work of Jesus Christ. In essence, God interprets our humanity through the blood-stained lens of what Jesus accomplished on Calvary's cross through his death, burial, and resurrection. Paul said in Philippians 3:13 (NIV), "Brothers and sisters, I do not consider myself yet to have taken hold of it. But

one thing I do: Forgetting what is behind and straining toward what is ahead." Your past may be questionable, but your future is secure in Jesus Christ's glory!

- **Guideline 4.** The righteous person releases power through prayer. The term powerful means having great strength. An example of this power being released through prayer is James 5:17 (NLT). There we find these words, "Elijah was as human as we are, and yet when he prayed earnestly that no rain would fall, none fell for three and a half years!" God saw his heart and answered his prayer. A word that describes one of God's attributes is *immutability.* In essence, God does not change. What he did for Elijah, he will do for you.
- **Guideline 5.** The righteous person is effective in prayer. The term effective means successful in producing a desired or intended result. Elijah prayed a second time to God knowing that he was all powerful. The outcome of his prayer is contained in James 5:18 (NIV): "Again he prayed, and the heavens gave rain, and the earth produced its crops." One person praying in a world consisting of seven billion people can get God's attention with earnest prayer. Is that person you?

Spend ten minutes today praying earnestly to God for your brothers and sister around the world for the purpose of releasing his sovereign grace in their lives. Decide to embrace prayer, the essential ingredient in lifestyle design. Think about it!

Day 25
Meditating on a New Thought Exercise

Reflection Thought: Your past may be questionable, but your future is secure in Jesus Christ's glory!

Principle to Remember: One person praying in a world consisting of seven billion people can get God's attention with earnest prayer.

Question to Explore: What are some issues that you can confess to a brother or sister today for the purpose of them seeking God on your behalf?

___

___

___

THEME 6

Philosophical Foundations

Day 26

Real-Life Ministry

In Hebrews 13:2 (NASB), we find these words: "Do not neglect to show hospitality to strangers, for by this some have entertained angels without knowing it." At the various intersections of our comings and goings, we often find ourselves in the company of strangers. I recall one night very vividly when I encountered a stranger that I would never forget. I was at a fast-food chain, studying information from an Introduction to Business class I was enrolled in at the time, when I encountered him. He asked me for a ride and said he had money. I usually don't give strangers a ride because it really isn't safe considering the level of violence that is so prevalent in our society. But for some strange reason, known only to me, I said, "Let's do this." He reeked of cigarette smoke, used profanity about every fifth word, and had trouble remembering where he needed to go. He attempted to light one up, and I said "I don't smoke, and secondhand smoke is not good. Please don't light that up." In essence, this person depicted carnality in its full representation. After several missed turns and an abrupt U-turn, we finally arrived at our destination of what seemed like twenty minutes of driving. In an instant, he was out the door without a thank you or offer to compensate me for gas. It seemed so rehearsed, as if he had done this before. To be truly honest, I felt used!

As I contemplated the situation, God helped me understand several important insights. True ministry forces us to encounter individuals who often don't look like us, who don't smell as nice, and who use profanity-laced language. When considering the life of Christ, emphatically I could see how he may have felt used by a corrupt society. His life of good actions and pure motives culminated on the cross next to two thieves and ended in death. Fortunately for us, there was eventual resurrection! My final conclusion concerning this situation is this: if we seek to engage in true ministry, we are likely to encounter individuals with habits and lifestyles characterized by secular tendencies. Secondly, sometimes the good we do will be met with indifference and a lack of appreciation. The question that we must all answer is this: "Are we up for the challenge?" I will be wondering from now until eternity if this was one of God's angels, better known as Homeboy!

Spend ten minutes asking God to increase your compassion for all humanity. Decide today to embrace real-life ministry. Think about it!

Day 26
Meditating on a New Thought Exercise

Reflection Thought: The ability to meet a person where they are and give them what they need is the essence of true ministry.

Principle to Remember: True ministry forces us to encounter individuals who often don't look like us, who don't smell as nice, and who use profanity-laced language.

Question to Explore: What is the motive for ministry in your life? Is it to obtain a monetary end or to give as you have freely received the gift of salvation?

____

____

____

Day 27

Scripture the Foundation of Effective Lifestyle Design

The apostle Paul said in 2 Timothy 3:16 (NIV), "All Scripture is God-breathed and is useful for teaching, rebuking, correcting and training in righteousness." Scripture provides five facts that serve as foundational elements in the lifestyle-design process. Scripture is God-breathed, or inspired. As stated by 2 Peter 1:21 (NIV), "For prophecy never had its origin in the human will, but prophets, though human, spoke from God as they were carried along by the Holy Spirit." God's plan was to always share his thoughts with his people. As you read the sacred writings contained in scripture, you are reading the very heart of an almighty God. Scripture teaches us how to have hope. According to Romans 15:4 (KJV), "For everything that was written in the past was written to teach us, so that through the endurance taught in the scriptures and the encouragement they provide we might have hope." It is only when you read about Paul—understanding that he could do all things through Christ, who gave him strength—that you begin to look at your life differently. Suddenly, your problem is transformed into an opportunity for God to reveal his power in your life.

Scripture rebukes the actions of the believer. The term rebukes means to express sharp disapproval or criticism. Reading and meditating on scripture is like looking into a mirror as you stand bare and undressed of all superficiality. The mirror reflects only the content of what is presented in front of it. As you begin to see yourself for who you truly are, you can then allow God to come in and make the necessary changes. Scripture corrects wrong beliefs and attitudes. The best correction comes from that small voice inside your heart, called your conscience. The best action is to stop and listen to what is being said. Scripture provides training in righteousness by dealing with the heart. Hebrews 4:12 (ESV) reveals, "For the word of God is alive and active. Sharper than any double-edged sword, it penetrates even to dividing soul and spirit, joints and marrow; it judges the thoughts and attitudes of the heart."

Spend ten minutes today studying scripture for the purpose of applying it to your life. Decide to embrace scripture, the foundation of effective lifestyle design. Think about it!

Day 27
Meditating on a New Thought Exercise

Reflection Thought: The realization of joy in daily living has to do with embracing the blessings you already have.

Principle to Remember: The best correction comes from that small voice inside your heart, called your conscience. The best action is to stop and listen to what is being said.

Question to Explore: What type of correction has your conscience been communicating that you need to change in your life?

____

____

____

Day 28

Thankfulness Expressed

The apostle Paul said in 1 Thessalonians 5:18 (NASB), "In everything give thanks; for this is God's will for you in Christ Jesus." It is easy to complain about what you do not have. It takes concerted effort to constantly thank God for what you do have. The simple act of thanking God every day for your family, friends, and career can totally transform your life. I suggest that you develop what I call a *gratitude list.* The importance of developing a gratitude list is an essential component in cultivating an atmosphere of thankfulness in your life. The gratitude list changes the focus from the things you don't have and proactively names, one by one, the many blessings that God has showered into your life.

The first step in developing the gratitude list is to think about the many wonderful blessings with which God has blessed you. If you were simply to sit down and make a list of everything you are thankful for, you would likely be blown away by how long your list becomes. The second step involves saying thank you to God by acknowledging his divine provision. This simple act exposes our dependence on him. It is at the point of dependency that we find his amazing grace.

Spend ten minutes today writing your thank-you list and expressing it to God. This is his will for you in Christ Jesus. Decide to embrace thankfulness expressed. Think about it!

Day 28
Meditating on a New Thought Exercise

Reflection Thought: Developing a gratitude list is an essential component in cultivating an attitude of gratitude.

Principle to Remember: Saying thank you to God acknowledges his divine provision in our lives.

Question to Explore: What are five things that you can put on your gratitude list today?

____

____

____

DAY 29

The Importance of Vision

The writer of Hebrews conveyed in Hebrews 11:1 (KJV), "Now faith is the substance of things hoped for, the evidence of things not seen." Individuals that subscribe to Christianity must possess faith in order to worship and serve an almighty God. Paul supports the idea that faith is substantial, embraces the concept of hope, and provides evidence for things we cannot yet see. Faith is substantial, or of considerable importance. In a world based on sight, faith allows an individual to act even when the circumstances do not support the actions being taken.

God told Noah to build an ark despite the fact there was dry ground all around him. Noah simply stepped out and faith predicated on obedience to God. When the rain came, Noah and his family rose to higher heights. Faith embraces the concept of hope. Hope is defined as a feeling of expectation and a desire for certain things to happen. In Nehemiah 8:10, we find these words (NIV): "For the joy of the LORD is your strength." Joy has a way of producing hope in our lives. The hope that we can become all that God has put into our hearts is a vital component of faith. Faith provides evidence for things we cannot yet see. In nature, we see faith at work every day. Every apple tree starts out as a seed. By faith, farmers drop the little seed into the ground with the expectation that one day, they will be eating an apple from an apple tree. Jesus declared in Matthew 17:20 that faith the size of a mustard seed could move mountains. As you apply your faith in expectation of great things, realize that the journey of a thousand miles begins with a single step. In other words, start planning for the business long before you sell your first product.

Spend ten minutes today designing your preferred destiny by faith. Develop that business plan, pick out a title for that song, and write the first stanza in your poem. Decide today to embrace the importance of vision. Think about it!

Day 29

Meditating on a New Thought Exercise

Reflection Thought: Faith embraces the concept of hope; it was hope that gave Nehemiah strength.

Principle to Remember: In a world based on sight, faith allows an individual to act even when the circumstances do not support the actions being taken.

Question to Explore: What is an area of your life where you need to apply faith today?

____

____

____

Day 30

The Jeremiah Paradigm

Jeremiah the Prophet writes these words concerning his life in Jeremiah 1:5 (KJV): "Before I formed you in the womb I knew you, before you were born I set you apart; I appointed you as a prophet to the nations." This portion of scripture allows us to listen like a fly on the wall, as Jeremiah recounts the revelation he received from God during the early days of his ministry. Learning from those that have gone before us is a great way to learn how God works in the human condition. As we examine the life of Jeremiah, we must understand three fundamental truths, presented here as what I refer to as the *Jeremiah paradigm*. A paradigm is a typical example or pattern of something, a model. The model that we want to briefly demonstrate relates to the purpose expressed in Jeremiah's life. Purpose, or the reason for which something is done or created, is paramount in your quest to live a fulfilling life. The first point we learn from the Jeremiah paradigm is that your purpose predates your conception. Notice the veracity of this truth contained in Psalm 139:16 (NIV): "Your eyes saw my unformed body; all the days ordained for me were written in your book before one of them came to be."

The second point we learn is that your purpose determines the occasion for your birth. Notice these words found in Jeremiah 29:11 (NIV): "For I know the plans I have for you," declares the LORD," plans to prosper you and not to harm you, plans to give you hope and a future. God knew you intimately before you were conceived. Your conception serves as an occasion for you to know him intimately after you are born.

The third point we learn is that your purpose is determined by God. Most people seek to develop a purpose after they are born, yet wise people understand that they simply discover the purpose God has already placed within! The circumstances surrounding your birth may be less than desirable; however, God's plan for your life has been determined.

Spend ten minutes today seeking God for insight concerning his plan for your life. Thank him for the talents and gifts that he has blessed you with. Decide today to embrace the *Jeremiah paradigm*. Think about it!

Day 30

Meditating on a New Thought Exercise

Reflection Thought: God knew you intimately before you were conceived. Your conception serves as an occasion for you to know him intimately after you are born.

Principle to Remember: Most people seek to develop a purpose after they are born, yet wise people understand that they simply discover the purpose God has already placed within!

Question to Explore: What do you feel is your purpose for existing?

____

____

____

Theme 7

Power for Living

Day 31

The Power of a Dream

Colin Powell said, "A dream doesn't become reality through magic; it takes sweat, determination and hard work." While dreams might not become reality as a result of magic, the dream itself has magical powers. A dream, or the ability to contemplate the possibility of doing something great, is therapeutic. In 1954, Roger Bannister became the first runner to eclipse the four-minute mile mark, a barrier that seemed impossible to break. What emerged as an outward reality for all the world to see evolved as an inner reality, depicted as a dream to Roger. After he accomplished the feat of running a four-minute mile, many runners followed suit. The hope of what can be is a prerequisite to doing great thing with your life. As you seek to express intrapersonal leadership by becoming skilled at leading yourself, remember this: the only place success comes before work is in the dictionary. Indeed, it will take sweat, determination, and hard work to make your dream a reality. Typically, as we advance chronologically, our propensity for dreaming is hijacked by the urgencies of life. What we must all do is dream more and envision a preferred future reality. Day by day, we must work hard until our hard work shows up in the form of a dream that originally started out as an embryonic thought.

Spend ten minutes today dreaming as you did when you were a kid and when all things were possible. Decide today to embrace the power of your dream as a prerequisite for intrapersonal leadership! Think about it!

Day 31
Meditating on a New Thought Exercise

Reflection Thought: While dreams might not become reality as a result of magic, the dream itself has magical powers.

Principle to Remember: The only place success comes before work is in the dictionary.

Question to Explore: What is one thing that you can do today to turn your dream into reality?

____

____

____

Day 32

The Power of Faith in The Creation Release Process

The writer of Hebrews said in Hebrews 13:1 (NIV), "Now faith is confidence in what we hope for and assurance about what we do not see." The power of faith cannot be underestimated in your quest to experience *creation release.* As we examine the concept of creation release, let's start with an adequate definition by defining the two words that comprise the term. Creation is the act of bringing something into existence. Release is defined as allowing or enabling something to escape from confinement or to be set free. *Creation release* then, is the process of bringing our greatness into existence and then setting it free into our external environment. As we approach Hebrews 13:1, faith becomes a prerequisite for discovering and releasing your greatness during your life experience. Faith is defined as complete trust or confidence in someone or something. As Christians, our confidence, hope, and trust reside in God alone. As you begin to understand who he is, then you begin to hear his still, small voice calling you to your greatness. You will experience newfound hope. Hope, or the feeling of expectation and desire for a certain thing to happen, begins to permeate your soul. The great thing that happens is that you began to sense your authentic self. God's intrinsic message to you is complete with assurance. Assurance is a positive declaration intended to give confidence.

In Jeremiah 1:5 (KJV), we find these beautiful words: "Before I formed you in the womb I knew you, before you were born I set you apart; I appointed you as a prophet to the nations." It is believed that Jeremiah was between the ages of thirteen and fourteen when he started his ministry. If this belief is true, he was a teenager in a grown man's world. He needed assurance from God that the greatness of a prophet resided within the essence of who he was. The words he received that day from God forever shaped his ministry as he faced days filled with tears and moments characterized by threats on his life. Despite the demands he faced, Jeremiah went on to become one of the major prophets of the Old Testament. He touched his inner greatness with the hands of faith and released it into his world for all humanity to see.

Spend ten minutes today touching your greatness with your hands of faith. To a musician, this looks like practice on scales. If you are a speaker or lecturer, it is working on your speech. It is only then that you define your greatness and only then that you will be allowed to release it into your world! Decide today to embrace the power of faith in the creation-release process. Think about it!

Day 32
Meditating on a New Thought Exercise

Reflection Thought: Creation release then, is the process of bringing our greatness into existence and then setting it free into our external environment.

Principle to Remember: As Christians, our confidence, hope, and trust reside in God alone.

Question to Explore: What has God placed inside of you that needs to be released?

____
____
____

Day 33

The Power of Joy

These remarkable words are found in Psalms 47:1 (ESV): "Clap your hands, all peoples! Shout to God with loud songs of joy!" It is important to involve your whole body in the act of creative worship. The Jewish understanding of worship embraces the idea that one's entire way of life is an expression of worship. The obvious outcome of creative worship is joy. Nehemiah communicates a truth that is as relevant today as it was when he proclaimed this amazing fact in Nehemiah 8:9 (NIV): "The Joy of the Lord Is Your Strength." In God's economy, joy equals strength, while lack of joy equals weakness. Joy does not depend on being happy as a validating factor. In real life, this looks like being deeply in debt yet feeling joyful because you realize that this too will pass. Joy is like a beacon of light that guides your every step during the darkness of the night. Joy does not deny the fact that it is dark. It simply provides the light of hope that shows you where to take your next step.

Spend ten minutes today worshiping God with your entire triune being. Simply raise your hands and shout, "The joy of the Lord is my strength!" Decide to embrace the power of joy!

Day 33
Meditating on a New Thought Exercise

Reflection Thought: Joy does not depend on being happy as a validating factor.

Principle to Remember: Joy does not deny the fact that it is dark. It simply provides the light of hope that shows you where to take your next step.

Question to Explore: What is one thing that you can be joyful about today?

____

____

____

Day 34

The Power of Love

Martin Luther King said, "Hatred paralyzes life; love releases it. Hatred confuses life; love harmonizes it. Hatred darkens life; love illuminates it." In your quest to realize your destiny, you will be required to pass the love test. Many of us come from circumstances characterized by physical abuse, poverty, and dysfunctional families. Many years later, we find ourselves locked in a prison called unforgiveness. We struggle to find joy in life because so much of our time is consumed with reliving the hurt that our victimizer imposed upon us, particularly if you come into contact with that person on a daily basis. Do yourself a favor by freeing your heart from the prison of unforgiveness. Take a chance and choose to love. When we chose to express love over hate, we experience life over death. Love is the most powerful force on earth. Choose today to express love in a variety of different ways. The one who will benefit the most is you!

Spend ten minutes making a decision to express love to someone who has hurt you in the past for the purpose of opening your heart to love again. Decide to embrace the power of love. Think about it!

Day 34
Meditating on a New Thought Exercise

Reflection Thought: When we chose to express love over hate, we experience life over death.

Principle to Remember: Many of us come from circumstances characterized by physical abuse, poverty, and dysfunctional families. Many years later, we find ourselves locked in a prison call unforgiveness.

Question to Explore: What one person do you need to forgive so that you can walk in love?

____

____

____

Day 35

The Power of Teamwork

Vince Lombardi said, "Individual commitment to a group effort—that is what makes a teamwork, a company work, a society work, a civilization work." In America, we live in what social scientists refer to as an individualistic society, where personal achievement is emphasized regardless of the expense to group goals resulting in a strong sense of competition. In collectivist cultures, such as China, Korea, and Japan, they emphasize family and work group goals above individual needs and desires. Each cultural dynamic has its strengths and weakness; however, the value of teamwork can never be overlooked. In fact, I want you to consider a three-step process for enhancing teamwork in your respective area of influence.

- **Step 1.** Consider your skill set by listing your strengths, talents, and abilities on paper.
- **Step 2.** Project yourself, releasing your skillset into your family, community, and society at large.
- **Step 3.** Find a group of individuals that possess similar goals, values, and energy as you do, and then engage in a dynamic called synergy. Synergy, in short, means the sum total of all the skills, talents, and abilities of the group members working together and producing a product that no one person of that group could produce. An individual can move some things in his or her world. A committed group of individuals can move the world.

Spend ten minutes developing plans to engage in teamwork with friends, family, or co-workers to accomplish a goal that improves the lives of all involved. Decide to embrace the power of teamwork! Think about it!

Day 35
Meditating on a New Thought Exercise

Reflection Thought: In America, we live in an individualistic society were individual goals are valued over group goals.

Principle to Remember: An individual can move some things in his or her world. A committed group of individuals can move the world.

Question to Explore: What talents and skills can you bring to your family or community?

___

___

___

THEME 8

Principles for Living

Day 36

The Principle of Multiplication

The apostle Matthew said in Matthew 25:18 (ESV), "But he who had received the one talent went and dug in the ground and hid his master's money." This concise scripture reference teaches us about the *principle of multiplication*. It is important to note the outcome of the Parable of the Talents, found in Matthew 25:14–30 and Luke 19:12–28. The servant that buried his one talent in the ground was exiled into darkness, where he gnashed his teeth. His talent was given to the servant who increased his talents from five to ten. As we consider the relevance of this parable, specifically as it relates to being proactive, there are several facts that combine synergistically to provide an educational moment for us. In the first place, our life from God is a gift; however, what we do with our lives is a gift back to God. God expects his people to contribute to the good of his kingdom by being productive. Every person arrives on this planet with at least one talent. The choice then becomes quite clear as we meander through the various decades of our lives. Either we choose to bury our talent in aimless diversion, or we proactively release it into our external environment, where it can multiply. Those really are the two choices that we have.

Another point we should observe: we will be held responsible for how we used our talents in life. As you project an image of yourself into that future date, how will you respond to our Lord and Savior concerning the stewardship of your talent? Did you hide it in the ground of mediocrity and complacency, or did you wake up with passion every day, with the intention of releasing your talent into your external environment for the purpose of multiplication? From this moment forward, you get the opportunity to answer that question with how you live your life each day.

The final point we want to examine is this: Scripture does not reveal how the two servants increased their talents to four and ten; however, we do know it was predicated on the skill set they came into the world with.

Spend ten minutes today assessing your skillset and then proactively starting the process of releasing your talent into your external environment. Decide today to embrace the principle of multiplication. Think about it!

Day 36

Meditating on a New Thought Exercise

Reflection Thought: God expects his people to contribute to the good of his kingdom by being productive.

Principle to Remember: Our life from God is a gift; however, what we do with our lives is a gift back to God.

Question to Explore: What gift will you present to God as an outcome of your life?

____

____

____

Day 37

The Principle of Study

The apostle Paul said in 2 Timothy 2:15 (KJV), "Study to shew thyself approved unto God, a workman that needeth not to be ashamed, rightly dividing the word of truth." Study (the devotion of time and attention to acquiring knowledge) is paramount in your life as a Christian living in the twenty-first century. In the mentor-mentee relationship that Paul had with his protégé, Timothy, the concept of study emerged as a relevant theme. I believe that Paul understood the importance of study, as a result of his chronological history. Later, God revealed the reason for Paul's extensive training and study, and he used him to write two-thirds of the New Testament. As we examine this portion of scripture, there are several ideas that we can ascertain.

The first point that Paul is making centers on the importance of studying to know God. In the life of the believer, what God has already written, through the personalities of about forty individuals, serves as the foundation of the faith-building process. As the reader meanders through the 929 chapters of the Old Testament and the 260 chapters of the New Testament, for a total of 1189 chapters, they, through that process of study, come to the knowledge of who God is.

The second point Paul is making centers on the idea of being competent or proficient in God's word. The Christian who attempts to stand on the foundation of humanism or philosophy has decided to build their house on sand. It only when one studies the word of God systematically that the antonym of *ashamed* is achieved—in other words, one is *proud* of an almighty God. Lastly, the idea of rightly dividing the word of truth involves the full application of God's wisdom in our everyday life. Paul understood that this was a necessary ingredient in fighting the good faith of faith.

Spend ten minutes today systematically studying God's word to apply his truth to your life. Decide today to embrace the principle of study. Think about it!

Day 37
Meditating on a New Thought Exercise

Reflection Thought: In the life of the believer, what God has already written through the personalities of about forty individuals serves as the foundation of the faith-building process.

Principle to Remember: The Christian who attempts to stand on the foundation of humanism or philosophy has decided to build their house on sand. It only when one studies the word of God systematically that the antonym of *ashamed* is achieved—in other words, one is *proud* of an almighty God.

Question to Explore: What have you learned in your current study of the Bible?

____

____

____

Day 38

Sight Without Vision

Helen Keller offered a glimpse of reality when she said, "The only thing worse than being blind is having sight but no vision." The world is full people who fail to ascertain the beauty of their own precious souls and as a result fail to maximize their potential. Having sight but no vision devalues your own worth, minimizes your future, and limits your ability to tap into the greatness that resides inside of you.

Having sight but no vision devalues your own worth. Vision or the ability to think about or plan the future with imagination or wisdom is a primary tool in taking your life purpose from idea to conception. Simply to live and exhaust the resources of life is really no life at all. The graveyards are filled with individuals that lived, paid their bills, and died without ever realizing their true potential. When you devalue or reduce your true greatness, I believe you live in desperation and chaos.

Having sight but no vision minimizes your future. I am reminded of how they train fleas in the South. As the story goes, fleas that are placed in a jar with a lid on it bump their heads until they learn to jump to a height that it just below the lid. This keeps them from hitting their heads on the lid, but it also keeps them from jumping to their full potential. Many of us operate in a similar fashion when we fail to truly appreciate our full worth. We jump just high enough to equate our effort with maintaining the status quo, and as a result never as high as we were intended to jump.

Having sight but no vision limits your ability to tap into the greatness that resides inside of you. This is perhaps the greatest peril associated with limited vision. While your parents, friends, and love one care about your future, no one should care about your future more than you. A concept called learned helplessness depicts a group of people that have been stripped of their volitional prowess and over time have become dependent on the geopolitical systems that govern their worldview. In essence, they exchange the responsibility of cultivating self-actualization for a government benefit.

Spend ten minutes today visualizing your future, because until you can see it, it is doubtful that you will achieve it. Decide today to embrace sight without vision. Think about it!

Day 38
Meditating on a New Thought Exercise

Reflection Thought: Having sight but no vision devalues our own worth.

Principle to Remember: Having sight but no vision limits your ability to tap into the greatness that resides inside of you.

Question to Explore: What is one action step that you can take today that will improve your vision for your future success?

____

____

____

Day 39

The Problem with Worrying

Benjamin Franklin said, "Do not anticipate trouble, or worry about what may never happen. Keep in the sunlight." It is important to develop the habit of not worrying about the future. Several psychologists suggest that 90 percent of the things people worry about never actually happen. Worrying about things that never happen affects you emotionally and robs you of the energy you need to solve problems in your current day. Instead of worrying, live each moment one at a time. Effectively handle the business of each day and laugh as you walk in the sunlight of productive living! Remember, most people fail in life because they fail to plan.

Spend ten minutes developing a plan to attack a problem that you are dealing with. Decide to understand the problem with worrying. Think about it!

Day 39

Meditating on a New Thought Exercise

Reflection Thought: The realization of joy in daily living has to do with embracing the blessings you already have.

Principle to Remember: Several psychologists suggest that 90 percent of the things people worry about never actually happen.

Question to Explore: What is one thing that you need to stop worrying about?

___

___

___

Day 40

The Value of Wisdom and Good Judgment

King Solomon said in Proverbs 4:7 (NLT), "Getting wisdom is the wisest thing you can do! And whatever else you do, develop good judgment." As we conclude the theme of being proficient, King Solomon offers us a template for success. The first element he offers has to do with obtaining wisdom or the quality of having experience, knowledge, and common sense. Proverbs 9:10 reveals, "The fear of the LORD is the beginning of wisdom, and knowledge of the Holy One is understanding." As you seek to become proficient in your quest for destiny acquisition as a Christian living in the twenty-first century, your foundation (or source) for true wisdom is reverence for God.

The second element that Solomon offers is the idea of having good judgment. Judgment (the ability to make considered decisions or to come to sensible conclusions) is a skill you will develop throughout your life's experience. Proverbs 24:16 (NIV) reminds us, "For though the righteous fall seven times, they rise again." It is often the hardest and most difficult experiences in life that teach us wisdom and good judgment. As you navigate the various experiences of your life, remember this: life is not so much what happens to you as it is what you decide to do with what happens to you.

Spend ten minutes today evaluating your life experiences and writing down the lessons you have learned. Translate that data into an educational moment by teaching the next generation to see life through the wisdom of your eyes. Decide today to embrace the value of wisdom and good judgment.

Day 40
Meditating on a New Thought Exercise

Reflection Thought: As you seek to become proficient in your quest for destiny acquisition as a Christian living in the twenty-first century, your foundation (or source) for true wisdom is reverence for God.

Principle to Remember: Life is not so much what happens to you as it is what you decide to do with what happens to you.

Question to Explore: What is one thing you need to let go of today that has been holding you back from progressing in life?

____
____
____

CONCLUSION

In the previous chapters we addressed eight themes supported by forty subsequent writings. I developed Thoughts for Your Day for the purpose of helping individuals develop an empowering thought life filled with purpose and possibility. Your thoughts can either liberate you, or they can keep you captive. The Apostle Paul exhorts his readers in Philippians 4:8 (NIV), "Finally, brethren, whatsoever things are true, whatsoever things *are* honest, whatsoever things *are* just, whatsoever things *are* pure, whatsoever things *are* lovely, whatsoever things *are* of good report; if *there be* any virtue, and if *there be* any praise, think on these things." My hope is that you have begun the process of liberation from old ways of thinking, past failures, and poor choices. Remember, life is not so much what has happened to you as it is what you do with what has happened to you. Change your thoughts, change your life! Think about it!

Three-Step Information Integration Tool

Principle to Commit to Memory

In our current social context as Christians, it is easy to get caught up in keeping up with the Jones and owning the latest high-tech cell phone, thus losing our foundation for living. Solomon teaches us that God is the true source of happiness and fulfillment.

1. Read the Principle
2. Write the Principle
3. Speak the Principle

Each time you write the principle, cross off each number, starting with the number 1, in the current set starting with the first set. For each set, you have ten repetitions to complete. After you complete the first set of ten, move to the next set of ten. Continue the process until you have committed the principle to memory. Obviously, this serves as an example, which you can adapt to fit your personal objectives as it relates to memorizing the various Scriptural reference and quotes contained in the text.

12345678910 12345678910 12345678910
12345678910 12345678910 12345678910

____
____
____

Expanded Quote, Principle, and Scripture Index

Principle Index

Theme 1: Self-Actualization

1. While some opportunities may repeat themselves over time, other opportunities only come once in a lifetime, so we must seize the moment.
2. You matter, and so does every right thing you do!
3. You were created with greatness built into the fabric of your essence.
4. Some of us are so busy walking hastily around the rose garden of life that we fail to stop and smell the roses.

5. A person without goals is like a map without detail—both will lead you to nowhere.

Theme 2: The Power of Friendship

1. As you consider the importance of choosing wise friends, ask God to give you the wisdom to fill your life with quality individuals with highly developed personalities.
2. Certain people enter our lives who possess the quality of friendship, and we are so much better because of them.
3. True friendship has an eternal component that transcends the natural and is really supernatural, because two hearts find the rhythm of life and beat as one.
4. Deleting assumed friends from your psychological capacity is a lot like deleting friends from Facebook. You still speak and smile when you see them, but they no longer have access to your important information.
5. Communication is key in understanding what constitutes a deposit for the person you are in a friendship with.

Theme 3: Goal Setting

1. Everything you need to be successful is programmed into the essence of who you are.
2. The problem for most of us is that we don't shoot at all and we hit! Low goals are a slam dunk!
3. When you write your goal down, you are enlisting both your conscious and unconscious mind to pay attention and focus in on your goals, thus harnessing the powers of concentration.
4. The vision you hold in your heart of the final outcome will serve as fuel to propel you through those tough days.
5. A person does not have to be physically dead to be dead in relation to their destiny.

Theme 4: Random Thoughts

1. While many rely on their own strength and skill to produce an outcome, Jesus relied on the strength of his father to fulfill his destiny.
2. The body was created for movement and totally regenerates each of its cells about every seven years.
3. As we approach each moment with an attitude of gratitude, we unleash the spirit of humility.
4. It's something about operating in a comfort zone that is appealing, since most people are creatures of habit. Yet, the people that changed the world refused to operate in comfort zones but continually embraced uncomfortable zones that pushed them into self-actualization.

Theme 5: Life Perspectives

1. The ability to manage spare moments will change your life.
2. Many people live their entire lives feeling like failures because they could never live up to the expectations of their parents, teachers, and important members of a specific group.
3. Choosing to love in the face of violence is character in motion.
4. On your deathbed, you are not going to wish you had spent a few extra hours at the office! You will probably wish you had spent more hours cultivating relationships with those you love.
5. One person praying in a world consisting of seven billion people can get God's attention with earnest prayer.

Theme 6: Philosophical Foundations

1. True ministry forces us to encounter individuals that often don't look like us, who don't smell as nice as we do, or who use profanity-laced language.

2. The best correction comes from that small voice inside your heart, called your conscience. The best action is to stop and listen to what is being said.
3. Saying thank you to God acknowledges his divine provision in our lives.
4. In a world based on sight, faith allows an individual to act even when the circumstances do not support the actions being taken.
5. Most people seek to develop a purpose after they are born. Yet wise people understand they simply discover the purpose God has already placed within!

Theme 7: Power for Living

1. The only place success comes before work is in the dictionary.
2. As Christians, our confidence, hope, and trust reside in God alone.
3. Joy does not deny the fact that it is dark. It simply provides the light of hope that shows you where to take your next step.
4. Many of us come from circumstances characterized by physical abuse, poverty, and dysfunctional families. Many years later, we find ourselves locked in a prison call unforgiveness.
5. An individual can move some things in his or her world. A committed group of individuals can move the world.

Theme 8: Principles for Living

1. Our life from God is a gift; however, what we do with our lives is a gift back to God.
2. The Christian who attempts to stand on the foundation of humanism or philosophy has decided to build their house on sand. It only when one studies the word of God systematically that the antonym of *ashamed* is achieved—namely, to simply be *proud* of an almighty God.
3. Having sight but no vision limits your ability to tap into the greatness that resides inside of you.

4. Several psychologists suggest that 90 percent of the things people worry about never actually happen.
5. Life is not so much what happens to you as it is what you decide to do with what happens to you.

Quote Index

Theme 1: Self-Actualization

1. Helen Keller said, "Life is short, eat your dessert first!"
2. Martin Luther King said, "I believe that unarmed truth and unconditional love will have the final word in reality. That is why right, temporarily defeated, is stronger than evil triumphant."—Nobel Peace Prize acceptance speech, December 10, 1964.
3. Earl Nightingale said, "People with goals succeed because they know where they're going."

Theme 2: The Power of Friendship

1. Marc Roberts said, "Friendship is a duality in motion, it is both spiritual and geographical simultaneously."
2. Aristotle said, "The antidote for fifty enemies is one friend."
3. An unknown author said, "Friendship isn't a big thing—it's a million little things."

Theme 3: Goal Setting

1. T. S. Eliot said, "Only those who will risk going too far can possibly find out how far one can go." Baby eagles are forced to learn to fly.
2. Les Brown said, "Shoot for the moon. Even if you miss, you'll land among the stars."
3. Sidney Howard said, "Half of knowing what you want is knowing what you must give up before you get it."

Theme 4: Random Thoughts

1. Emily Dickinson said, "The mere sense of living is joy enough."
2. Albert Einstein said, "Insanity: doing the same thing over and over again and expecting different results."

Theme 5: Life Perspectives

1. Ralph Waldo Emerson said, "Guard well your spare moments. They are like uncut diamonds. Discard them and their value will never be known. Improve them and they will become the brightest gems in a useful life."
2. Albert Einstein said, "Try not to become a man of success, but rather try to become a man of value."
3. Martin Luther King said, "Returning violence for violence multiplies violence, adding deeper darkness to a night already devoid of stars. ... Hate cannot drive out hate: only love can do that."
4. Steven Covey said, "Start with the end in mind."

Theme 7: Power for Living

1. Colin Powell said, "A dream doesn't become reality through magic; it takes sweat, determination and hard work."
2. Martin Luther King said, "Hatred paralyzes life; love releases it. Hatred confuses life; love harmonizes it. Hatred darkens life; love illuminates it."
3. Vince Lombardi said, "Individual commitment to a group effort—that is what makes a team work, a company work, a society work, a civilization work."

Theme 8: Principles for Living

1. Benjamin Franklin said, "Do not anticipate trouble, or worry about what may never happen. Keep in the sunlight."

Scripture Index

Theme 1: Self Actualization

1. King Solomon says in Proverbs 20:5 (NIV), "The purposes of a person's heart are deep waters, but one who has insight draws them out."
2. King Solomon said in Proverbs 21:5 (NIV), "The plans of the diligent lead to profit as surely as haste leads to poverty."

Theme 2: The Power of Friendship

1. King Solomon said in Proverbs 13:20 (NIV), "He who walks with the wise grows wise, but a companion of fools suffers harms."
2. Samuel the seer provides us with important information related to the friendship of Jonathan and David in 1 Samuel 18:1 (ESV): "As soon as he had finished speaking to Saul, the soul of Jonathan was knit to the soul of David, and Jonathan loved him as his own soul."

Theme 3: Goal Setting

1. The prophet Habakkuk said in Habakkuk 2:2 (EAS), "And the LORD answered me: "Write the vision; make it plain on tablets, so he may run who reads it."
2. The apostle Paul said in Philippians 3:14 (NIV), "I press on toward the goal to win the prize for which God has called me heavenward in Christ Jesus."

Theme 4: Random Thoughts

1. In 2 Kings 13:21 we find these words: "Once while some Israelites were burying a man, suddenly they saw a band of raiders; so, they threw the man's body into Elisha's tomb. When the body touched Elisha's bones, the man came to life and stood up on his feet."

2. Jesus Christ said in Luke 22:42, "Father, if you are willing, take this cup from me; yet not my will, but yours be done."
3. The apostle Paul conveys in 1 Timothy 4:8, "For physical training is of some value, but godliness has value for all things, holding promise for both the present life and the life to come."

Theme 5 Life Perspectives

1. The apostle James said in James 5:16, "Therefore confess your sins to each other and pray for each other so that you may be healed. The prayer of a righteous person is powerful and effective. (NIV)"

Theme 6 Philosophical Foundations

1. In Hebrews 13:2, we find these words (NASB): "Do not neglect to show hospitality to strangers, for by this some have entertained angels without knowing it."
2. The apostle Paul said in 2 Timothy 3:16 (NIV), "All Scripture is God-breathed and is useful for teaching, rebuking, correcting and training in righteousness."
3. The apostle Paul said in 1 Thessalonians 5:18 (NASB), "In everything give thanks; for this is God's will for you in Christ Jesus."
4. The writer of Hebrews conveyed in Hebrews 11:1 (KJV), "Now faith is the substance of things hoped for, the evidence of things not seen."
5. Jeremiah the Prophet writes these words concerning his life in Jeremiah 1:5 (NIV): "Before I formed you in the womb I knew you, before you were born I set you apart; I appointed you as a prophet to the nations."

Theme 7: Power for Living

1. The writer of Hebrews said in Hebrews 13:1 (NIV), "Now faith is confidence in what we hope for and assurance about what we do not see."
2. These remarkable words are found in Psalms 47:1 (ESV): "Clap your hands, all peoples! Shout to God with loud songs of joy!"

Theme 8: Principles for Living

1. The apostle Matthew said in Matthew 25:18 (NSV), "But he who had received the one talent went and dug in the ground and hid his master's money."
2. The apostle Paul said in 2 Timothy 2:15 (KJV), "Study to shew thyself approved unto God, a workman that needeth not to be ashamed, rightly dividing the word of truth."
3. Apostle Luke writes in Luke 22:42 (NIV), "Father, if you are willing, take this cup from me; yet not my will, but yours be done."
4. King Solomon said in Proverbs 4:7 (NLT), "Getting wisdom is the wisest thing you can do! And whatever else you do, develop good judgment."

Printed in the United States
By Bookmasters